THE SEX GODDESS

HANDBOOK

How to Please a Man Sexually, Tease Him, Ride Him and Make Him Beg for More

By

Adam Vogler

TABLE OF CONTENTS

INTRODUCTION

Welcome to The Sex Goddess Handbook, a comprehensive guide to help you become an expert in pleasing your man sexually. This book is designed for women who want to enhance their sexual confidence, improve their skills in the bedroom, and have a more satisfying sexual relationship with their partner.

What is a Sex Goddess?
A Sex Goddess is a woman who is confident in her sexuality, knows what she wants and how to get it, and is skilled at giving and receiving sexual pleasure. She is not afraid to explore her desires and experiment with new techniques and positions in the bedroom. A Sex Goddess embodies the perfect combination of femininity, sensuality, and sexual prowess, making her partner feel desired, satisfied, and fulfilled.

Why Learn How to Please a Man Sexually?

Learning how to please a man sexually is not only about satisfying his physical desires but also about building a stronger emotional connection with him. Sexual intimacy is an important aspect of any relationship, and a lack of sexual satisfaction can lead to frustration, resentment, and even infidelity. By becoming a Sex Goddess, you will not only be able to give your man the pleasure he craves but also deepen your bond and strengthen your relationship.

Additionally, sexual confidence can have a positive impact on other areas of your life. It can boost your self-esteem, improve your communication skills, and enhance your overall well-being. When you feel confident and empowered in the bedroom, you radiate that confidence in other aspects of your life, leading to a more fulfilling and satisfying existence.

In this book, we will cover everything you need to know to become a Sex Goddess. From understanding male anatomy and psychology to exploring kinks and fantasies, you will gain the knowledge, skills, and confidence to give your man the ultimate sexual experience. So, let's begin this journey towards sexual empowerment and become the ultimate Sex Goddess.

CHAPTER ONE

Understanding Male Sexual Anatomy and Psychology

In order to become a Sex Goddess and please your man sexually, it is important to understand the male sexual anatomy and psychology. This knowledge will enable you to understand how men experience sexual pleasure and what turns them on.

Male Sexual Anatomy: What You Need to Know

Male sexual anatomy refers to the physical structures and organs that are involved in male sexual function and reproduction.

Understanding male sexual anatomy is essential for women who want to please their man sexually.

✓ **The penis** is the primary male sexual organ, and it has three main parts: the root, the shaft, and the glans. The root of the penis is located inside the pelvis and is attached to the pubic bone. The shaft is the long, cylindrical part of the penis that extends from the root to the tip. The glans is the rounded head of the penis that is located at the tip of the shaft.
The penis contains two main chambers, known as the corpora cavernosa, which are responsible for producing an erection. The urethra, which is the tube that carries urine and semen out of the body, runs through the center of the penis.

✓ **The scrotum** is the pouch of skin that contains the testicles, which are responsible for producing sperm and the male sex hormone testosterone. The testicles are sensitive to touch and can be a source of pleasure when stimulated.

✓ **The Testicles:** The testicles are the two egg-shaped organs located in the scrotum. They are responsible for producing and storing sperm, as well as producing testosterone, the male sex hormone.

✓ **The prostate gland** is another essential part of male sexual anatomy, located just below the bladder. The prostate gland produces some of the fluid that makes up semen and is also responsible for controlling the flow of urine.

Understanding male sexual anatomy is essential for women who want to please their man sexually. By learning about the different parts of the male sexual anatomy, women can better understand how to stimulate their partner and help them achieve sexual satisfaction. Additionally, understanding male sexual anatomy can also help women identify potential issues or concerns related to sexual function and seek appropriate medical care if needed.

The Male Sexual Response Cycle

The male sexual response cycle is a series of physiological and psychological changes that occur during sexual activity. It is composed of four phases: excitement, plateau, orgasm, and resolution.

✓ **Excitement Phase:** During the excitement phase, the man's body responds to sexual stimuli, such as touch or visual cues. Blood flow to the penis increases, causing an erection.

✓ **Plateau Phase:** In the plateau phase, the man's arousal level continues to increase, and his body prepares for ejaculation. Breathing and heart rate increase, and muscle tension increases.

✓ **Orgasm Phase:** The orgasm phase is the peak of sexual pleasure, during which the man experiences ejaculation and a release of sexual tension. This is accompanied by feelings of pleasure and euphoria.

✓ **Resolution Phase:** The resolution phase is the final phase of the male sexual response cycle. The man's body returns to its normal state, and the sexual tension dissipates.

Common Male Sexual Fantasies and Desires

Men have a wide range of sexual fantasies and desires, which can vary from person to person. However, some common male sexual fantasies and desires include oral sex, anal sex, and dominance/submission. Understanding your partner's desires and fantasies can help you provide the sexual experiences that he craves.

Here are some additional examples:

1. Threesome: This is a common male fantasy that involves having sex with two women or with another man and a woman.

2. Voyeurism: Some men enjoy watching their partner engage in sexual activities with someone else or even watching strangers have sex.

3. BDSM: Bondage and discipline, dominance and submission, and sadism and masochism are all common components of BDSM. Many men find pleasure in being dominant or submissive, or in being restrained or otherwise controlled during sexual activity.

4. Exhibitionism: This is the desire to be seen by others while engaging in sexual activity, such as having sex in a public place or being watched by a partner.

5. Roleplay: Some men enjoy playing out sexual fantasies or scenarios with their partner, such as pretending to be a doctor and patient or teacher and student.

It is important to note that these fantasies and desires are not exclusive to men and can be shared by women as well. The key to a satisfying sexual relationship is to communicate openly and honestly with your partner about your desires and boundaries.

How to Communicate About Sex With Your Partner

Effective communication is crucial for a satisfying sexual relationship. It is important to establish a safe and open environment in which you and your partner can discuss your sexual desires and preferences. This can involve discussing likes and dislikes, exploring new techniques, and establishing boundaries. Good communication can lead to a deeper understanding of each other's needs and desires, and can ultimately enhance your sexual relationship.

Here are some tips on how to communicate about sex with your partner:

1. Create a safe and open environment: It is important to establish a safe and open environment in which you and your partner can discuss your sexual desires and preferences. This can involve establishing trust, respect, and mutual understanding.

2. Start the conversation: Sometimes, the hardest part of communication is getting started. Begin by expressing your desires and asking your partner about theirs. Be honest and non-judgmental in your approach.

3. Listen actively: It is important to listen actively to your partner's desires and needs. Pay attention to their body language, tone of voice, and facial expressions. Encourage them to be honest and open about what they want and need.

4. Explore new techniques: Try new techniques and positions together. Be open to experimenting and exploring each other's desires.

5. Establish boundaries: It is important to establish boundaries and respect each other's limits. Discuss what is and is not acceptable behavior and ensure that both partners feel comfortable and safe.

By communicating effectively about sex, you and your partner can enhance your sexual relationship and build a stronger emotional connection. Remember, good communication takes practice and patience, but the rewards are worth it.

CHAPTER 2

Building Sexual Confidence and Becoming a Sex Goddess

Sexual confidence is an essential ingredient to please a man sexually. When you feel confident in your own skin and are comfortable with your own sexuality, it becomes easier to communicate with your partner about your desires and needs, and to explore new techniques and experiences together. In this chapter, we will discuss how to build sexual confidence and become a sex goddess.

Embracing Your Sexuality

The first step towards building sexual confidence is to embrace your own sexuality. This involves understanding and accepting your body, your desires, and your sexual preferences. You can start by exploring your own body and learning what feels good to you. Experiment with masturbation and try different techniques to discover what turns you on.

It is also important to understand that everyone's sexuality is unique and there is no one "right" way to express your sexuality. Embrace your own desires and preferences, and don't be afraid to communicate them to your partner.

Developing Sexual Confidence

Sexual confidence is not something that you are born with; it is something that you can develop over time. Here are some tips on how to develop sexual confidence:

✓ **Practice self-care:** Taking care of yourself physically and emotionally can help you feel more confident and comfortable with your own sexuality. Exercise regularly, eat a healthy diet, and practice stress-reducing techniques such as meditation or yoga.

✓ **Educate yourself:** Learning about sex and sexual techniques can help you feel more confident in the bedroom. Read books, watch educational videos, or attend workshops or classes on sexuality.

✓ **Practice communication**: Effective communication is key to building sexual confidence. Practice communicating your desires and needs with your partner in a non-judgmental and open way.

✓ **Explore new experiences**: Trying new experiences, techniques, and positions can help you feel more confident in your own sexuality. Be open to experimentation and new experiences.

How to Be Confident in Bed

Being confident in bed involves feeling comfortable with your own body and sexuality, and being able to communicate effectively with your partner. Here are some tips on how to be confident in bed:

✓ **Focus on pleasure**: Instead of worrying about how you look or what you are doing, focus on the pleasure that you are giving and receiving. Pay attention to your partner's reactions and respond to their cues.

✓ **Take charge**: Being confident in bed also involves taking charge of your own sexual experiences. Don't be afraid to initiate sex, communicate your desires and needs, and try new things.

✓ **Be present**: Be present in the moment and focus on the physical sensations and emotions that you are experiencing. Don't get distracted by self-doubt or negative thoughts.

The Power of Sexual Energy

The power of sexual energy is a fascinating topic that has been explored in various spiritual and philosophical traditions for centuries. In recent years, scientific research has also shed light on the benefits of tapping into one's sexual energy for overall well-being and happiness.

At its core, sexual energy is the life force energy that flows through every human being. This energy is the source of our sexual desire, passion, and pleasure, but it also plays a significant role in our overall physical and emotional health.

One way to tap into your sexual energy is through mindfulness and meditation practices. These practices can help you become more aware of your own physical sensations and emotions, and teach you how to channel your sexual energy in positive ways. This can lead to increased sexual confidence and enhanced sexual experiences, as well as a sense of overall well-being and connection to yourself and others.

In addition, tapping into your sexual energy can also have other health benefits. Research has shown that regular sexual activity can lead to decreased stress levels, improved immune function, and even a longer lifespan.

Furthermore, by embracing your sexual energy, you can also develop a greater sense of self-awareness and self-acceptance. You can learn to appreciate your own body and desires, and become more confident and comfortable with your own sexuality. This can lead to better communication with your partner and a more fulfilling sex life.

In conclusion, the power of sexual energy is a powerful force that can enhance your overall well-being and quality of life. By tapping into your own sexual energy, you can become a more confident and empowered sexual partner, and experience a deeper connection with yourself and others.

CHAPTER 3

The Art of Seduction: How to Turn Your Man On

When it comes to pleasing a man sexually, seduction is a key element that cannot be overlooked. In this chapter, we will explore the art of seduction and provide you with tips and techniques for turning your man on and building sexual tension.

The Importance of Foreplay

Foreplay is a critical aspect of sexual intimacy that is often overlooked or rushed. It is the time and attention given to sexual arousal and physical stimulation before engaging in intercourse. Foreplay can consist of a variety of activities, including kissing, touching, massaging, and oral sex.

The importance of foreplay cannot be overstated when it comes to pleasing a man sexually. It is a crucial element of sexual intimacy that can enhance pleasure, increase sexual desire and arousal, and create a stronger emotional connection between partners.

During foreplay, the body prepares for sexual intercourse by increasing blood flow to the genitals, which causes them to become engorged and more sensitive to touch. This increased sensitivity can lead to more intense and pleasurable sexual experiences.

Additionally, foreplay can be a great way to build intimacy and emotional connection between partners. It allows for time and space to explore each other's bodies, desires, and preferences, and can help partners feel more comfortable and connected during sex.

It's important to note that foreplay does not have to be a specific set of actions or a prescribed length of time. Rather, it is about taking the time to explore and enjoy each other's bodies, and paying attention to your partner's reactions and desires.

How to Seduce Your Man

Seduction is a process that involves building sexual tension and creating anticipation, ultimately leading to a more intimate and pleasurable sexual experience. Here are some tips on how to seduce your man:

✓ **Dress to impress:** Wearing something that makes you feel confident and sexy can be a powerful tool in seduction. Choose clothing that accentuates your best features and makes you feel comfortable and confident.

✓ **Flirt:** Flirting involves playful and suggestive communication that creates a sense of attraction and desire. Use compliments, jokes, and playful banter to create a sense of connection and attraction between you and your partner.

✓ **Touch:** Physical touch is an essential part of seduction. Start with light, playful touches, such as a gentle touch on the arm or a caress on the back of the neck. Gradually increase the intensity and duration of your touches to build sexual tension.

✓ **Use your body language:** Your body language can communicate a lot about your intentions and desires. Use eye contact, facial expressions, and gestures to convey your interest and desire for your partner.

✓ **Create a romantic atmosphere:** Setting the mood can be an essential part of seduction. Light candles, play soft music, and create a comfortable and intimate environment to help your partner relax and feel more comfortable.

✓ **Tease:** Teasing can be a powerful tool in building sexual tension and creating anticipation. Playfully tease your partner by withholding physical or verbal cues, creating a sense of anticipation and desire.

Techniques for Building Sexual Tension

Building sexual tension is another important aspect of seduction. This can be achieved through teasing and withholding, such as stopping a sexual act before it reaches its peak, and then resuming later. You can also try incorporating new and unexpected elements into your sexual routine, such as trying new positions or incorporating sex toys. Here are some techniques for building sexual tension:

✓ **Tease with your words:** Using suggestive language and dirty talk can be a powerful tool in building sexual tension. Talk about your desires and fantasies, and use your words to create a sense of anticipation and desire.

✓ **Play hard to get:** Playing hard to get can create a sense of challenge and excitement, making your partner want you even more. Use teasing, flirting, and suggestive body language to create a sense of anticipation and desire.

✓ **Use eye contact:** Eye contact can be a powerful tool in building sexual tension. Use prolonged eye contact to communicate your desire and attraction, and create a sense of intimacy and connection.

✓ **Touch strategically:** Touching your partner in strategic places can be a powerful tool in building sexual tension. Use light, playful touches on erogenous zones such as the neck, ears, and inner thighs to create a sense of arousal and desire.

✓ **Use props and accessories:** Props and accessories, such as blindfolds, handcuffs, or lingerie, can be a fun and exciting way to build sexual tension and create a sense of anticipation.

✓ **Take it slow:** Taking your time and building sexual tension gradually can be a powerful tool in creating a more intimate and pleasurable sexual experience. Use foreplay and teasing to build anticipation and desire, and gradually increase the intensity and duration of your physical contact.

Using Your Body Language to Turn Your Man On

Finally, your body language can play a significant role in turning your man on. Use eye contact, touch, and body positioning to communicate your desires and build sexual tension. For example, leaning in close and whispering in your partner's ear can be a highly effective way to turn them on.

Here are some tips on how to use your body language to turn your man on:

✓ **Eye contact:** Maintaining eye contact with your partner can be a powerful tool in building sexual tension and communicating your desire. Use prolonged eye contact to convey your attraction and desire for your partner.

✓ **Smiling:** Smiling is a natural way to communicate your attraction and interest in your partner. A warm, inviting smile can help put your partner at ease and create a sense of intimacy and connection.

✓ **Touching:** Touching your partner in a suggestive or playful way can be a powerful way to communicate your desire and attraction. Use light, playful touches on erogenous zones such as the neck, ears, and inner thighs to create a sense of arousal and desire.

✓ **Posture:** Good posture can be a subtle yet effective way to convey confidence and sexual attractiveness. Stand up straight and hold your head high to convey confidence and sexual desirability.

✓ **Lip biting:** Biting your lip can be a subtle yet suggestive way to convey your sexual desire and attraction. Use this technique sparingly, as it can quickly become overdone and lose its impact.

✓ **Slow movements:** Slow, deliberate movements can be a powerful tool in building sexual tension and creating a sense of anticipation and desire. Use slow, deliberate movements to convey your confidence and sexual desirability.

In conclusion, the art of seduction is an essential element in pleasing a man sexually. By understanding the importance of foreplay, using effective seduction techniques, building sexual tension, and using your body language, you can enhance your sexual experiences and strengthen your relationship with your partner.

CHAPTER 4

Techniques for Pleasing Your Man Sexually

In this chapter, we will explore some of the most effective techniques for pleasing your man sexually. From oral sex to handjobs, we will cover a variety of techniques that are sure to leave your partner feeling satisfied and fulfilled.

Oral Sex: Techniques for Giving Great Head

Oral sex is a powerful tool in any sexual arsenal, and mastering the art of giving great head can be a game-changer in the bedroom.

Here are some tips on how to give great oral sex:

✓ **Start slow:** Take your time and explore your partner's body with your mouth and tongue. Use slow, sensual movements to build anticipation and pleasure.

✓ **Pay attention to the tip:** The head of the penis is the most sensitive area, so pay special attention to it. Use your tongue to circle the tip and tease your partner with gentle licks and kisses.

✓ **Use your hands:** Don't be afraid to use your hands to enhance the experience. Use your hands to stroke and caress your partner's thighs and hips, or use them to cup and fondle his testicles.

✓ **Experiment with different techniques:** Every person is different, so don't be afraid to experiment with different techniques to find out what works best for your partner. Try using different tongue movements or varying the pressure and speed of your strokes.

Handjobs: How to Make Him Melt

Handjobs are a classic technique for pleasing your partner and can be a great way to switch things up in the bedroom. Here are some tips on how to give an amazing handjob:

✓ **Use lube:** Lube can make the experience more comfortable and pleasurable for your partner. Choose a high-quality, water-based lube for the best results.

✓ **Use your hands creatively:** Don't be afraid to get creative with your hands and experiment with different techniques. Try using one hand to stroke the shaft while using the other to massage the testicles, or use your thumb to massage the frenulum.

✓ **Build up the intensity:** Start slow and gradually build up the intensity to increase your partner's pleasure. Use different strokes and techniques to keep things interesting.

✓ **Pay attention to his reactions:** Pay attention to your partner's reactions and adjust your technique accordingly. If he seems to be enjoying a particular stroke or technique, keep doing it.

Positions for Ultimate Pleasure

Experimenting with different sexual positions can be a great way to enhance your sexual experience and bring you and your partner closer together. Here are some positions to try:

✓ **Missionary:** This classic position allows for deep penetration and intimate eye contact.

✓ **Doggy style:** This position is great for hitting the G-spot and allows for deep penetration from behind.

✓ **Cowgirl:** This position allows for more control and can be great for women who want to take charge.

✓ **The G-Whiz:** In this position, the woman lies on her back with her legs spread wide, while the man enters her from a kneeling position. This position allows for deep penetration and G-spot stimulation.

✓ **The Pearly Gates:** In this position, the woman lies on her back with her legs raised up, while the man enters her from a kneeling position. This position allows for deep penetration and easy access to the clitoris.

✓ **The Leap Frog:** In this position, the woman gets on all fours, while the man enters her from behind. This position allows for deep penetration and G-spot stimulation.

✓ **The Butter Churner:** In this position, the woman lies on her back with her legs raised and crossed, while the man enters her from a kneeling position. This position allows for deep penetration and G-spot stimulation.

✓ **The Coital Alignment Technique:** In this position, the woman lies on her back with her legs raised, while the man enters her from a kneeling position. The man then shifts his hips forward so that his pubic bone presses against the woman's clitoris for increased stimulation.

✓ **The X Marks the Spot:** In this position, the woman lies on her back with her legs spread wide, while the man enters her from a kneeling position. The man then crosses his legs to form an "X" and thrusts in and out.

✓ **The Lotus:** In this position, the woman sits on top of the man with her legs wrapped around his waist, while the man enters her.

This position allows for intimate face-to-face contact and clitoral stimulation.

✓ **The Viennese Oyster:** In this position, the woman lies on her back with her legs raised and pulled towards her head, while the man enters her from a kneeling position. This position allows for deep penetration and G-spot stimulation.

✓ **The CAT Position:** Similar to the Coital Alignment Technique, the woman lies on her back with her legs raised, while the man enters her from a kneeling position. The man then shifts his hips forward and up, so that his penis rubs against the clitoris for increased stimulation.

✓ **The Crab:** In this position, the woman sits on the edge of a bed or chair with her legs spread wide, while the man enters her from a standing position. This position allows for deep penetration and G-spot stimulation.

✓ **The Standing Wheelbarrow:** In this position, the woman stands facing a wall or surface with her hands on the surface for support, while the man enters her from behind. This position allows for deep penetration and clitoral stimulation.

✓ **The Lap Dance:** In this position, the woman sits on the man's lap facing him, while he enters her. This position allows for intimate face-to-face contact and clitoral stimulation.

✓ **The Spork:** In this position, the woman lies on her back with her legs spread wide, while the man enters her from a kneeling position. The man then lifts one of the woman's legs and holds it up for increased penetration and G-spot stimulation.

✓ **The Amazon:** In this position, the woman straddles the man with her back facing him, while he enters her. This position allows for deep penetration and G-spot stimulation.

✓ **The Reverse Cowgirl:** In this position, the woman straddles the man facing away from him, while he enters her. This position allows for deep penetration and G-spot stimulation.

Prostate Play: How to Stimulate His Prostate

Prostate play, also known as prostate massage or milking, can be an incredibly pleasurable experience for many men. The prostate is a gland located just inside the rectum, and when stimulated, it can produce intense sensations and even lead to orgasm.

Before attempting prostate play, it's important to have a conversation with your partner about their boundaries and preferences. Some men may not be interested in this type of stimulation, while others may require a specific type of touch or pressure to enjoy it.

To begin, make sure that both you and your partner are relaxed and comfortable. Use plenty of lube and slowly insert a well-lubricated finger into the rectum. The prostate will feel like a small, round bump about 2-3 inches inside the rectum.

Once you've located the prostate, experiment with different types of touch and pressure. Some men prefer a light, tapping motion, while others may enjoy a more firm pressure or circular motion. Pay attention to your partner's reactions and adjust your touch accordingly.

You can also experiment with using toys designed specifically for prostate stimulation, such as prostate massagers or vibrating toys. Again, communication is key - make sure that your partner is comfortable and enjoying the experience.

It's important to note that prostate play should never be painful or uncomfortable. If your partner experiences any discomfort or pain, stop immediately and check in with them. With patience, communication, and a willingness to explore, prostate play can be a highly pleasurable and intimate experience for both partners.

CHAPTER 5

Exploring Kinks and Fantasies

Sexual exploration and experimentation can be exciting and fulfilling, especially when it comes to exploring kinks and fantasies. Kinks and fetishes are specific sexual interests that are outside of what is considered "normal" or "vanilla" sexual activity. In this chapter, we will explore the world of kinks and fetishes, and how to explore them safely with your man.

Understanding Kinks and Fetishes

Kinks and fetishes are not something to be ashamed of. In fact, they are very common and can add excitement and pleasure to your sex life. It is important to understand what your kinks and fetishes are, and to communicate them clearly with your partner.

A kink is a specific sexual interest that is outside of what is considered "normal" sexual activity. For example, some people have a foot fetish, which means they are sexually aroused by feet. Other common kinks include bondage, dominance and submission, and roleplay.

Fetishes are more specific than kinks and often involve a particular object or body part. For example, a person with a leather fetish may be aroused by the sight or touch of leather.

How to Talk About Kinks With Your Partner

Talking about your kinks and fetishes with your partner can be nerve-wracking, but it is important to have open and honest communication about what you both like and don't like. Here are some tips for talking about kinks with your partner:

1. Choose the right time and place: Make sure you are both in a relaxed and private setting where you won't be interrupted.

2. Start small: Begin by talking about something you are both comfortable with and gradually work your way up to more taboo subjects.

3. Be respectful: It's important to respect your partner's boundaries and not judge them for their interests.

4. Listen: Make sure you actively listen to your partner and respond with empathy and understanding.

Common Kinks and How to Explore Them Safely

There are many different kinks and fetishes, and it is important to explore them safely and consensually. Here are some common kinks and how to explore them safely:

1. Bondage: This involves restraining your partner using ropes, cuffs, or other materials. Make sure to use safe and sturdy equipment, and always have a safe word in case things get too intense.

2. Dominance and submission: This involves one partner taking a dominant role and the other taking a submissive role. Always establish clear boundaries and use safe words to ensure both partners feel comfortable and safe.

3. Foot fetishes: This involves being sexually aroused by feet. Make sure to keep your feet clean and use safe and consensual methods of exploration.

4. Spanking: This involves spanking your partner's buttocks with your hand or a paddle. Always start slowly and gradually build up intensity, and make sure to use a safe word.

Using Roleplay to Spice Things Up

Roleplaying can be a fun and exciting way to explore your fantasies with your partner. When exploring roleplay, it's important to establish clear boundaries and use safe words to ensure both partners feel comfortable and safe.

To begin with, it's important to discuss your desires and boundaries with your partner before engaging in any kind of roleplay. This will ensure that you're both on the same page and comfortable with the scenario you're exploring.

Some common roleplay scenarios include teacher/student, boss/employee, doctor/patient, or even a classic maid/butler scenario. Whatever scenario you choose, the key is to fully commit to your role and immerse yourself in the fantasy.

In addition to assuming different roles, you can also incorporate costumes, props, and even dialogue to enhance the experience. For example, if you're playing a teacher/student scenario, you might wear a schoolgirl outfit and use a ruler as a prop.

The key to successful roleplay is to keep an open mind, be playful, and most importantly, have fun! Don't be afraid to experiment with different scenarios and explore your deepest desires with your partner. With the right attitude and approach, roleplay can be a fun and exciting way to keep the spark alive in your sex life.

CHAPTER 6

Keeping the Spark Alive: Tips for Long-Term Sexual Satisfaction

After you've mastered the art of seduction and pleasing your man sexually, the next challenge is to maintain sexual satisfaction in a long-term relationship. In this chapter, we'll explore some tips and techniques for keeping the spark alive and ensuring long-term sexual satisfaction.

How to Maintain Sexual Chemistry in a Long-Term Relationship

Maintaining sexual chemistry in a long-term relationship can be challenging, especially as the initial excitement and novelty of the relationship wear off. However, with a bit of effort and creativity, it's possible to keep the spark alive. Here are some tips:

✓ **Schedule regular date nights**: It's important to make time for each other and prioritize your relationship. Schedule regular date nights and make them a priority.

✓ **Communicate openly and honestly:** Communication is key in any relationship, and this is especially true when it comes to sexual satisfaction. Talk openly and honestly about your needs, desires, and fantasies.

✓ **Don't be afraid to try new things** and explore new fantasies together. This can help keep things fresh and exciting.

✓ **Take care of yourself:** It's important to take care of yourself both physically and emotionally. This can help you feel more confident and attractive, which can translate into a more satisfying sex life.

Common Sexual Issues in Women and How to Overcome Them

Even the happiest couples can experience sexual issues from time to time. Here are some common sexual issues and how to overcome them:

There are several common sexual issues that women may experience, including:

✓ **Lack of Desire**: Many women experience a decrease in sexual desire at some point in their lives, which can be caused by hormonal changes, stress, relationship issues, or other factors. To overcome this, it's important to identify the underlying cause and address it with the help of a healthcare professional, therapist, or sex therapist.

✓ **Pain During Sex:** Pain during sex, also known as dyspareunia, is a common problem that can be caused by a variety of factors, such as vaginal dryness, infections, hormonal imbalances, or pelvic floor dysfunction. Treatment options may include lubricants, hormone therapy, physical therapy, or other medical interventions.

✓ **Difficulty Achieving Orgasm**: Many women struggle to achieve orgasm during sex, which can be due to a variety of reasons, such as anxiety, relationship issues, or lack of knowledge about their own bodies. To overcome this, it's important to explore your own body and communicate your needs with your partner. You may also benefit from trying different sexual positions, using sex toys, or practicing mindfulness techniques to reduce anxiety.

✓**Body Image Issues:** Many women feel self-conscious about their bodies during sex, which can lead to decreased sexual confidence and satisfaction. To overcome this, it's important to practice self-love and acceptance, and focus on the pleasure you're experiencing rather than your appearance. You may also benefit from discussing your concerns with your partner and exploring new sexual positions that make you feel more comfortable.

✓**Communication Issues**: Communication is key to a healthy and satisfying sex life, but many women struggle to communicate their needs and desires with their partners. To overcome this, it's important to work on your communication skills and build trust with your partner. You may also benefit from exploring different communication techniques, such as nonverbal cues or written communication.

Overall, it's important to remember that sexual issues are common and can be overcome with the right approach and support. If you're experiencing any sexual issues, don't be afraid to reach out to a healthcare professional or sex therapist for help.

How to Keep Your Man Satisfied and Coming Back for More

Keeping your man satisfied sexually is key to a happy and healthy relationship. Here are some tips for keeping him coming back for more:

✓ **Show appreciation:** Let him know how much you appreciate him and the effort he puts into your relationship. This can help him feel more connected and satisfied.

✓ **Be spontaneous:** Surprise him with a sexy text message or a surprise visit to his office. This can help keep things exciting and fresh.

✓ **Experiment**: Don't be afraid to try new things and experiment with different techniques and positions. This can help keep your sex life exciting and satisfying.

✓ **Be confident:** Confidence is key when it comes to pleasing your man sexually. Don't be afraid to take the lead and show him what you want.

✓ **Communicate:** Communication is key in any relationship, especially when it comes to sex. Make sure to talk to your partner about what they like and don't like, and be open to trying new things.

✓ **Pay attention to his needs:** Make sure to focus on your partner's pleasure as well as your own. Ask him what he likes and be attentive to his responses.

✓ **Don't be afraid to take charge:** Sometimes, men enjoy when their partner takes control in the bedroom. Take charge and show your man what you want.

✓ **Keep the intimacy alive outside the bedroom:** Sexual satisfaction isn't just about what happens in the bedroom. Make sure to show your partner love and affection outside of sex as well. This will help to build a deeper connection and keep the spark alive.

Remember, keeping your man satisfied sexually is about more than just physical pleasure. It's about building a strong emotional connection and exploring new things together.

CONCLUSION

Congratulations, you have completed The Sex Goddess Handbook! This book has provided you with a wealth of knowledge and techniques for pleasing your man sexually. By embracing your sexuality, developing confidence, and exploring new techniques and fantasies, you can become a true sex goddess and keep your man satisfied and coming back for more.

The Importance of Sexual Empowerment
It's important to remember that being a sex goddess isn't just about pleasing your man. It's also about taking ownership of your sexuality and feeling empowered in the bedroom. By learning about your own desires and needs, you can communicate better with your partner and ensure that you are both getting what you want out of your sexual experiences.

Embrace Your Sexuality and Enjoy the Journey

Sex is a natural, healthy part of life, and it's important to enjoy it! Don't be afraid to explore new techniques, try new things, and indulge in your fantasies. With the knowledge and confidence you've gained from this book, you are well-equipped to become a true sex goddess and enjoy a fulfilling and satisfying sex life.

Remember, becoming a sex goddess takes practice, patience, and a willingness to learn and grow. But with the right attitude and approach, you can become the confident, sensual, and irresistible woman you've always wanted to be. So go forth, embrace your sexuality, and enjoy the journey!

Made in the USA
Coppell, TX
02 November 2024

39526168R00036